CHRISTMAS BOOK

LEVEL **2B**

P9-DNT-691

PIANO

Adventures® *by Nancy and Randall Faber*

THE BASIC PIANO METHOD

CONTENTS

About the "Sightreading Stocking Stuffers"

A student's enthusiasm for learning Christmas music can become an opportunity to create enthusiasm for sightreading. In this book, each Christmas song is presented with short melodies, called "Sightreading Stocking Stuffers."

The "Sightreading Stocking Stuffers" are **melodic variations** of the carol being studied. Teachers will notice that the lyrics and rhythm patterns are from the carol. By drawing on these familiar rhythms, the student may effectively focus on interval reading and note reading.

The student should sightread one "stocking stuffer" a day while learning the Christmas song. Or, the stocking stuffers can be used as sightreading during the lesson itself.

The teacher may wish to tell the student:

> **Sightreading means "reading music at first sight."**
>
> When sightreading, music is not practiced over and over. Instead, it is only played once or twice with the highest concentration.

The following **3 C's** may help the student with sightreading:

 CORRECT HAND POSITION
Find the correct starting note for each hand.

 COUNT - OFF
Set a steady tempo by counting one "free" measure before starting to play.

 CONCENTRATE
Focus your eyes on the music, carefully reading the intervals.

FF1140

Note to Teacher: This page reviews theory concepts in the keys of C and G, preparing the student for the carols and sightreading that follow.

Stuffing the Stockings

Draw a line connecting each "gift" to the correct stocking.

Teacher duet is at the bottom of p. 5.

Up on the Housetop

Cheerfully

**Words and Music by
Benjamin R. Hanby**

FF1140

The words to the "stocking stuffers" are familiar, but the **melodies have changed!**

Sightread one "stocking stuffer" a day while learning the carol. Your teacher may also ask you to transpose.

Circle the stocking after sightreading!

("variations" for sightreading)

DAY 1

mf
(Up on the house-top rein-deer pause.)

DAY 2

Can you transpose to G major?

mf
(Out jumps good old San-ta Claus.)

DAY 3

f
(Ho, ho, ho! Who would-n't go!)

DAY 4

Can you transpose to G major?

mf
(Down thru the chimney with good St. Nick!)

DAY 5 — In *Up on the Housetop,* put a ✔ above each measure that uses only notes of the C chord.

DAY 6 — In *Up on the Housetop,* circle each V7 chord.

Teacher Duet for p. 4: (Student plays *as written*)

BOTH HANDS 8va throughout

R.H.
L.H. *p*

p   *mp*   *f*

5

Joy to the World

Words by Isaac Watts
Music by G. F. Handel

FF1140

Sightread one "stocking stuffer" a day
while learning *Joy to the World*.

Circle the stocking after sightreading!

JOYOUS
STOCKING
STUFFERS
("variations" for sightreading)

Can you transpose to G major?

DAY 1

f (Joy   to   the   world!   The   Lord   is   come.)

DAY 2

(Let   earth   re - ceive   her   King.)

Can you transpose to D major?

DAY 3

mf (Let   ev - ery___   heart___   pre - pare___   Him___   room.___)

DAY 4

(And   heav'n and   na - ture___   sing,   and   heav'n and   na - ture___   sing.)
mp

DAY 5   In *Joy to the World,* find and circle a complete ascending C scale.

DAY 6   Draw the lowest note in *Joy to the World.*

Teacher duet is at the bottom of p. 9.

Mary Had a Baby

Spiritual

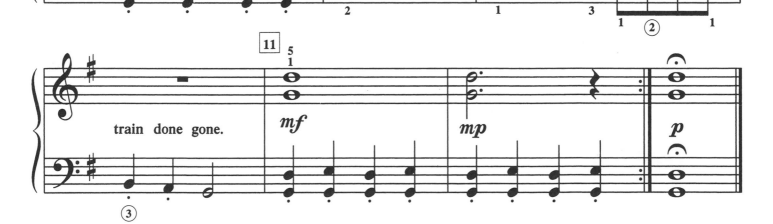

Additional Lyrics

2. What did she name Him?
3. She called Him Jesus,
4. Where was He born?

5. Born in a stable,
6. Where did they lay Him?
7. Laid Him in a manger,

Optional: The eighth notes may be played in a long-short swing rhythm. (♫ = ♩³♪)

8

Sightread one "stocking stuffer" a day
while learning *Mary Had a Baby.*

Circle the stocking after sightreading!

CHRISTMAS
STOCKING
STUFFERS

("variations" for sightreading)

DAY 1 — Can you transpose to C major?
(Mar-y had a Ba-by, Oh, Lord.___)

DAY 2 — Can you transpose to C major?
(Oh, Oh, my Lord._)

DAY 3 — Can you transpose to C major?
(Mar-y had a Ba-by, Oh, Lord.)

DAY 4 — Can you transpose to D major?

DAY 5 — Write the first measure for the L.H. in *Mary Had a Baby.*

DAY 6 — Transpose the first measure of *Mary Had a Baby* to the Key of C.

Teacher Duet for p. 8: (Student plays *as written*)

Teacher duet is at the bottom of p. 11.

Silent Night

Words by Joseph Mohr
Music by Franz Grüber

(echo softly)

Peacefully

Si - lent night, Ho - ly night,

All is calm, all is bright

'round yon vir - gin moth - er and Child.
Ho - ly In - fant so ten - der and mild,

repeat

Sleep in heav - en - ly peace.

L.H. ② *over*

L.H. ② *R.H.* 5

Sleep_____ in heav - en - ly peace.

L.H. ② *over*

Sightread one "stocking stuffer" a day
while learning *Silent Night.*

Circle the stocking after sightreading!

PEACEFUL STOCKING STUFFERS

("variations" for sightreading)

DAY 1

DAY 2

Can you transpose to G major?

Si - lent night.

All is calm.

DAY 3

DAY 4

Can you transpose to C? to D?

Ho - ly night.

DAY 5 In *Silent Night*, put a ✔ above
each measure with this rhythm:

DAY 6 Draw the highest note in *Silent Night.*

Teacher Duet for p. 10: (Student plays *1 octave higher*)

R.H.

L.H. *p*   *with pedal*   *pp*   *p*

8va

Jingle Bells

Words and Music by
J. Pierpont

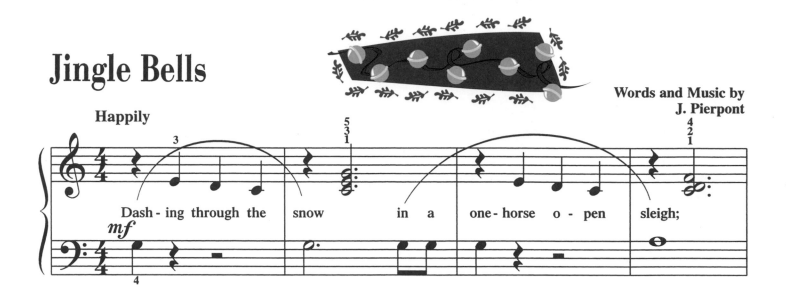

Happily

Dash - ing through the snow in a one - horse o - pen sleigh;

mf

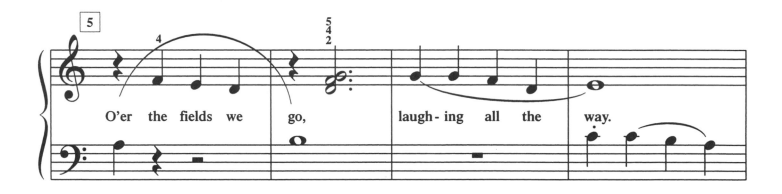

5

O'er the fields we go, laugh - ing all the way.

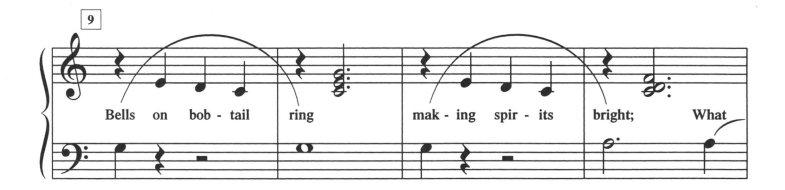

9

Bells on bob - tail ring mak - ing spir - its bright; What

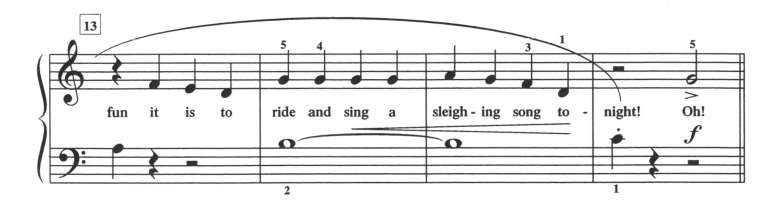

13

fun it is to ride and sing a sleigh - ing song to - night! Oh!

f

FF1140

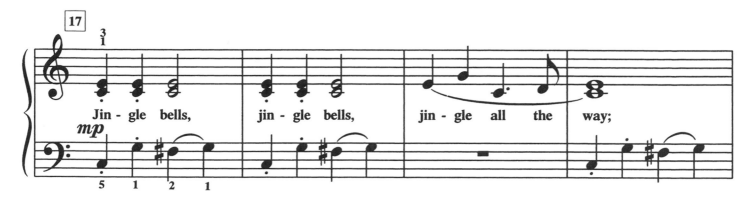

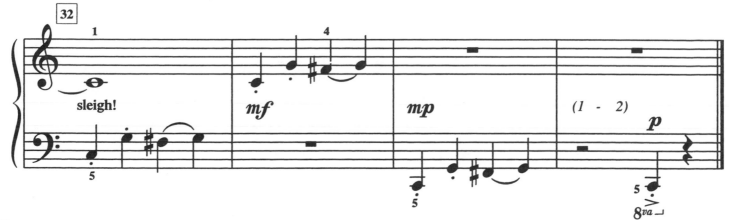

Sightread one "stocking stuffer" a day
while learning *Jingle Bells.*

Circle the stocking after sightreading!

SNOWY STOCKING STUFFERS

("variations" for sightreading)

Can you transpose to D major?

DAY 1

mp
(Jin - gle bells, jin - gle bells, jin - gle all the way.)

Can you transpose to G major?

DAY 2

mf
(Oh, what fun it is to ride in (a) one - horse o - pen sleigh!)

Can you transpose to D major?

DAY 3

(Jin - gle bells, jin - gle bells, *f* jin - gle all the way.)
mp

Can you transpose to G major?

DAY 4

mf
(Oh, what fun it is to ride in a one - horse o - pen sleigh!)

DAY 5 Copy the R.H. of measures 19-20 of
Jingle Bells. Use the staff below.

DAY 6 Now transpose the R.H. of
mm. 19-20 to the Key of G.

FF1140

Fingering Check: Practice the R.H. alone for correct fingering. Then play hands together.

What Child Is This?

Traditional English Tune

Gently

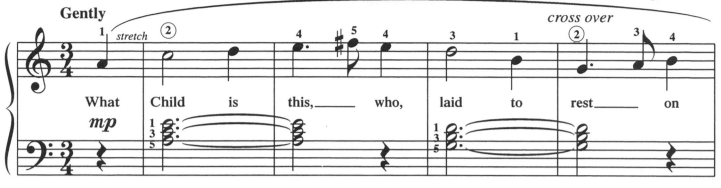

What Child is this,_____ who, laid to rest_____ on

mp

Mar - y's lap,_____ is sleep - ing? Whom

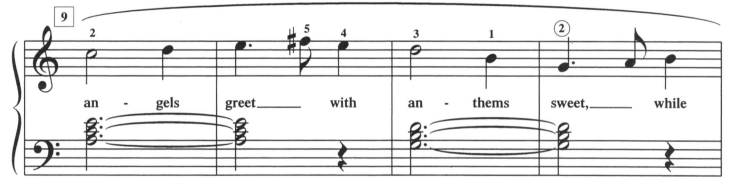

an - gels greet_____ with an - thems sweet,_____ while

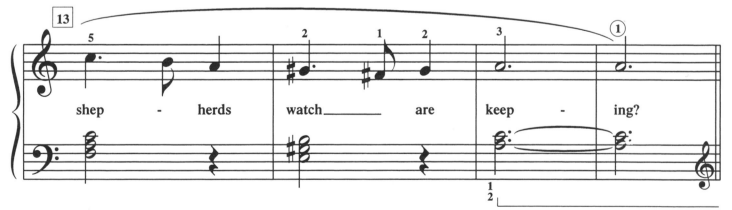

shep - herds watch_____ are keep - ing?

Teacher Duet: (Student plays *1 octave higher*)

R.H.

L.H. *p*
(teacher pedals on duet)

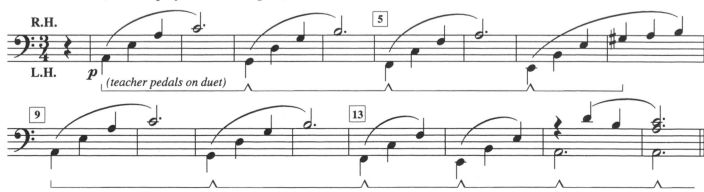

Sightread one "stocking stuffer" a day while learning *What Child Is This?*

Circle the stocking after sightreading!

OLD ENGLISH STOCKING STUFFERS

("variations" for sightreading)

Can you transpose to D minor?

DAY 1

mp

Can you transpose to G minor?

DAY 2

mf

DAY 3

mf

Can you transpose to D minor?

DAY 4

mp

DAY 5

In *What Child Is This*, put a ✔ above each measure with this rhythm:

DAY 6

Write the four chords used in *What Child Is This?*

A minor   G major   F major   E major

Deck the Halls

Brightly

Traditional

Deck the halls with boughs of hol - ly, }
'Tis the sea - son to be jol - ly, }
Fa la la la la, la

la la la.
Don we now our gay ap - par - el

Fa la la, la la la la la la, Troll the an - cient

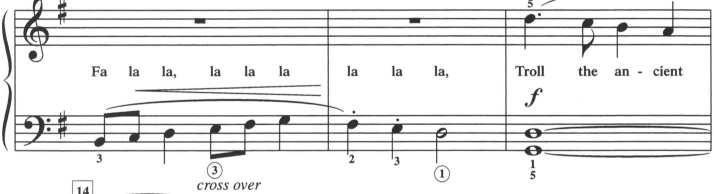

Yule - tide car - ol, Fa la la la la, la la la

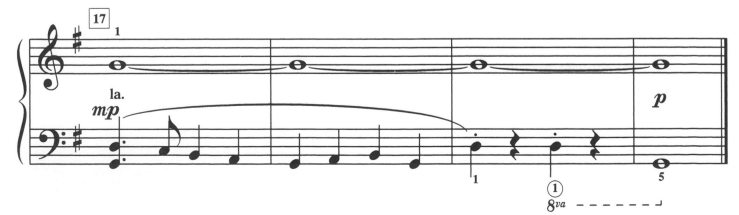

la.

FF1140

Sightread one "stocking stuffer" a day while learning *Deck the Halls.*

Circle the stocking after sightreading!

HOLLY STOCKING STUFFERS

("variations" for sightreading)

The Twelve Days of Christmas

Traditional

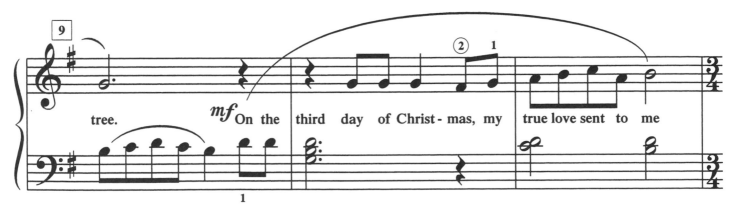

FF1140

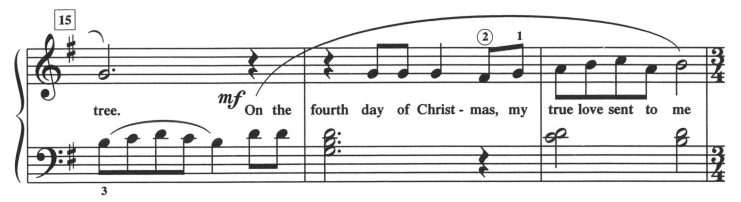

Sightread one "stocking stuffer" a day
while learning *The Twelve Days of Christmas.*

Circle the stocking after sightreading!

TURTLE DOVE
STOCKING
STUFFERS

("variations" for sightreading)

Can you transpose to C major?

DAY 1
(On the first day of Christ - mas, my true love sent to me.)

Can you transpose to D major?

DAY 2
(Two tur- tle doves, two tur- tle doves.)

Can you transpose to A major?

DAY 3
(Three French_ hens, two tur- tle doves, and a par- tridge_ in a pear tree.)

Can you transpose to C major?

DAY 4
(Four_ call - ing birds, three French hens, two_ tur- tle doves.)

DAY 5 Transpose the first 4 measures of *The Twelve Days of Christmas* to the Key of C?

DAY 6 There is one dotted quarter note in this piece. Can you find and circle it?

Christmas Music Calendar

Complete the music calendar for each day of December.

DEC. 1
Write the time signature for these stars.

DEC. 2
Draw a **quarter rest** in the holly leaf.

DEC. 3
Draw a **tie** connecting the notes.

DEC. 4
Draw a whole note a **6th above** the star.

DEC. 5
Draw a whole note a **6th below** the star.

DEC. 6
Draw a **half rest** on the top of the snowman.

DEC. 7
Draw a **repeat sign** after the present.

DEC. 8
Circle the key a **half step higher** than the candy cane.

DEC. 9
Circle the key a **whole step lower** than the candy cane.

DEC. 10
Circle the **leading tone** in the C scale.

C D E F G A B C

DEC. 11
Circle the **tonic** note in the G scale.

G A B C D E F♯ G

DEC. 12
Draw a **treble clef** in front of the bells.

DEC. 13
Draw two different **G's** on the bass staff.

DEC. 14
Draw a **natural** on the top of the tree.

DEC. 15
Circle the **dominant** note in the C scale.

C D E F G A B C

DEC. 16
Draw an **eighth rest** on the gift.

DEC. 17
Decorate the reindeer antlers with your favorite music symbols.

DEC. 18
Draw the symbol which shows the carolers singing **gradually louder**.

DEC. 19
Draw the symbol which shows the carolers singing **gradually softer**.

DEC. 20
Name the **key signature.**

Key of ___

DEC. 21
Write the **C** scale (C to C) on the staff below.

DEC. 22
Write the **G** scale (G to G) on the staff below.

DEC. 23
Write your own sleighbell rhythm in 𝄴 time below.

DEC. 24
Christmas Eve!
Draw 3 different **C's** (for *Celebrate Christmas Carols*) on the staff below. (Use whole notes).

DEC. 25
Christmas Day!
Play your favorite Christmas songs!